EXAMPLES OF GREGORIAN CHANT AND WORKS BY ORLANDUS LASSUS, GIOVANNI PIERLUIGI PALESTRINA AND MARC ANTONIO INGEGNERI

Crofts Books in Music

A HISTORY OF MUSICAL THOUGHT   By D. N. Ferguson

A SHORT HISTORY OF MUSIC   By D. N. Ferguson

THE ANALYSIS OF FORM IN MUSIC   By E. W. Doty

EASTMAN SCHOOL OF MUSIC SERIES

EXAMPLES ILLUSTRATING THE DEVELOPMENT OF MELODIC LINE AND CONTRAPUNTAL STYLE FROM GREEK MELODY TO MOZART
       By Gustave Fredric Soderlund

EXAMPLES OF GREGORIAN CHANT AND WORKS BY ORLANDUS LASSUS, GIOVANNI PIERLUIGI PALESTRINA, AND MARC ANTONIO INGEGNERI
       By Gustave Fredric Soderlund

METHOD OF ORGAN PLAYING   By Harold Gleason

A MODERN METHOD FOR THE DOUBLE BASS   By Nelson Watson

ANSWERS TO SOME VOCAL QUESTIONS   By Thomas Austin-Ball

HANDBOOK OF CONDUCTING   By Karl Van Hoesen

CHORALE COLLECTION   By Elvera Wonderlich

EXAMPLES OF MUSIC BEFORE 1400   By Harold Gleason

SIGHT-SINGING MANUAL   By Allen Irvine McHose & Ruth Northup Tibbs

DIRECT APPROACH TO COUNTERPOINT IN SIXTEENTH CENTURY STYLE
       By Gustave Fredric Soderlund

THE CONTRAPUNTAL HARMONIC TECHNIQUE OF THE EIGHTEENTH CENTURY
       By Allen Irvine McHose

BASIC PRINCIPLES OF THE TECHNIQUE OF 18TH AND 19TH CENTURY COMPOSITION (*In preparation*)   By Allen Irvine McHose

TEACHERS DICTATION MANUAL   By Allen Irvine McHose

KEYBOARD AND DICTATION MANUAL
       By Allen Irvine McHose and Donald F. White

Eastman School of Music Series

EXAMPLES OF GREGORIAN CHANT
and Works by
ORLANDUS LASSUS
Giovanni Pierluigi Palestrina
AND MARC ANTONIO INGEGNERI
for use in Classes of Counterpoint

THIRD EDITION

Compiled by

GUSTAVE FREDRIC SODERLUND

Theory Department, Eastman School of Music
University of Rochester

APPLETON-CENTURY-CROFTS, INC.
New York

FOREWORD TO THE FIRST EDITION

It has become increasingly apparent in the last few years that the study of counterpoint should begin with the technique of the later sixteenth century, as exemplified in the style of Palestrina. Since the secular compositions of this composer involve a great deal of melodic and harmonic freedom, I have, for the sake of greater pedagogic discipline, limited the choice of compositions in this compilation to the liturgical church music of Palestrina but have attempted to make the selection comprehensive enough for serious study.

Since a preliminary study of modal melody is essential, I have included a number of Gregorian chants. Some of these have been recorded phonographically by the monks of the Abbey of Solesmes.

The three offertories are recorded by the Vatican Choir.

I have also included as illustrations of writing in two parts, twelve Cantiones Duarum Vocum and a Benedictus by Orlandus Lassus.

To Dr. Howard Hanson, Director of the Eastman School of Music, who has made possible the publication of this compilation, and Miss Barbara Duncan, Librarian of the Sibley Musical Library, who gave me easy access to the necessary material, I give my sincerest thanks.

Gustave Fredric Soderlund.

Rochester, New York
March, 1937.

FOREWORD TO THE SECOND EDITION

The first edition of this compilation has proved to be exceedingly useful in classes of counterpoint in the Eastman School of Music as well as a number of other universities and colleges throughout the country.

The second edition, revised and enlarged, has been planned as an improvement on the first edition. By the addition of two complete masses, the L'Homme Armé and the Hexachord mass, as well as most of the canonic mass Repleatur os meum laude, a Litany, the eight-part motet O Admirabile Commercium, the twelve-part motet Laudate Dominum in Tympanis, and finally examples of Responses by Ingegneri illustrating modal homophonic treatment, the scope of the study of sixteenth-century ecclesiastical style has been considerably widened.

Another addition is a translation of all Latin texts contained in this volume.

Gustave. Fredric Soderlund

Rochester, New York
March, 1941

FOREWORD TO THE THIRD EDITION

The present — the third — edition, has been corrected and two compositions in triple time by Palestrina have been added: The motet Tollite jugum and the "Hosanna" from the mass O Regem Coeli.

Gustave Fredric Soderlund

Rochester, New York
October, 1946

CONTENTS

CONTENTS

Gregorian Chant.
(Alme Pater.)

2.

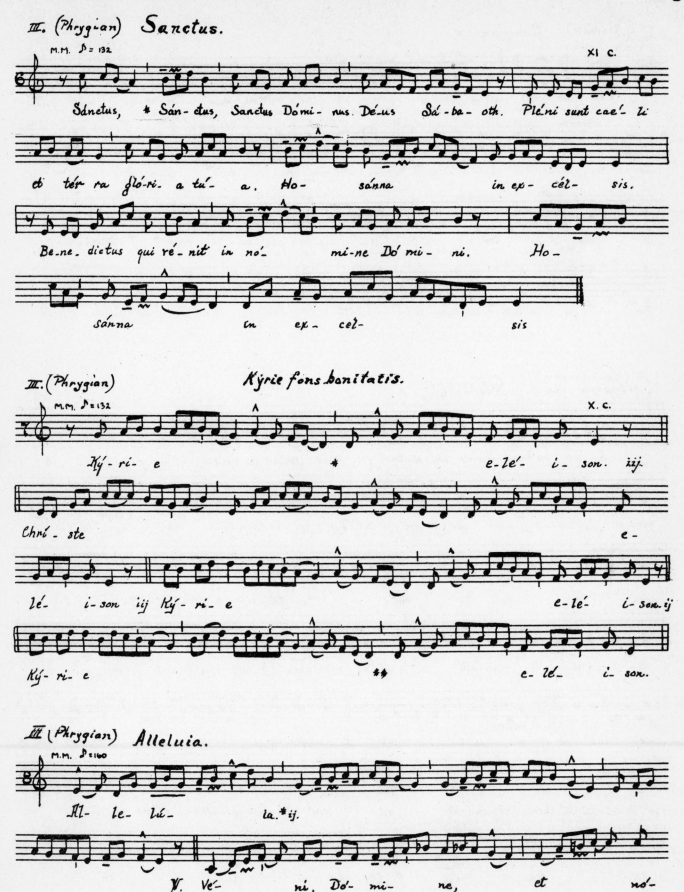

4.

-li tar-dá- re: re-lá- xa fa-ci-

no- ra * plé'-bis tu'- ae.

IV. (Hypophrygian) Response.

Ec- ce*quó'-mo-do mó'-ri-tur jú- stus, et né- mo pér- ci-pit

cór- de: et ri-ri jú-sti tol-lún- tur, et né- mo

con- sí- de- rat: a fa'-ci- e in-i-qui-ta- tis

sublá'- tus est jú- stus: * Et é'- rit in pá'-

ce me-mó'- ri- a é'- jus. V. Tamquam agnus co-ram ton-den-te

se ob-mú-tu-it, et non apé'-ru- it os sú- um: de an-gú'-sti- a, et de ju-di-ci-o

sublá'- tus est. * Et é'- rit. R. Ec- ce.

V. (Lydian) Sanctus.

M.M. ♪ = 116

XIV c.

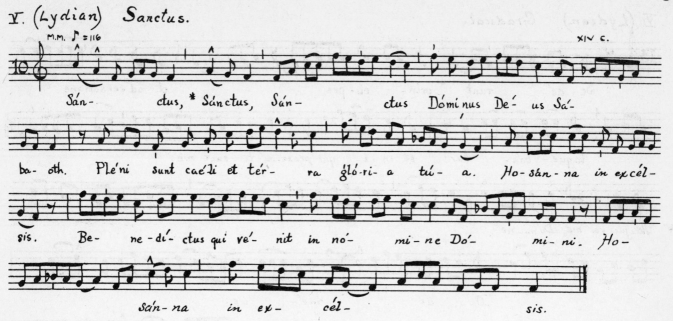

Sán- ctus, * Sánctus, Sán- ctus Dóminus Dé- us Sá-
ba- óth. Pléni sunt caéli et tér- ra glóri-a tú- a. Ho-sán- na in excél-
sis. Be- ne-dí-ctus qui ve'- nit in nó- mi-ne Do'- mi-ni. Ho-
sán- na in ex- cél- sis.

V. (Lydian) Agnus Dei.

M.M. ♪ = 132

(X) XIII c.

Ag- nus De'- i, * qui tól- lis pec-ca'- ta mún- di: mi-
se- re'- re no'- bis. Ag- nus De'- i, * qui tól- lis pecca'-ta mún-di:
mi- se- re'- re no'- bis: Ag- nus De'- i, * qui tól- lis pecca'- ta
mún- di: do'- na no'- bis pa'- cem.

V. (Lydian) Antiphon.

Ecce Do'-mi-nus re-ni-et,* et ómnes sáncti é-jus cum é- o: et é'-rit in di-e ll-la
lux má'gna, alle- lú'-ia. E- u o u a e.

6.

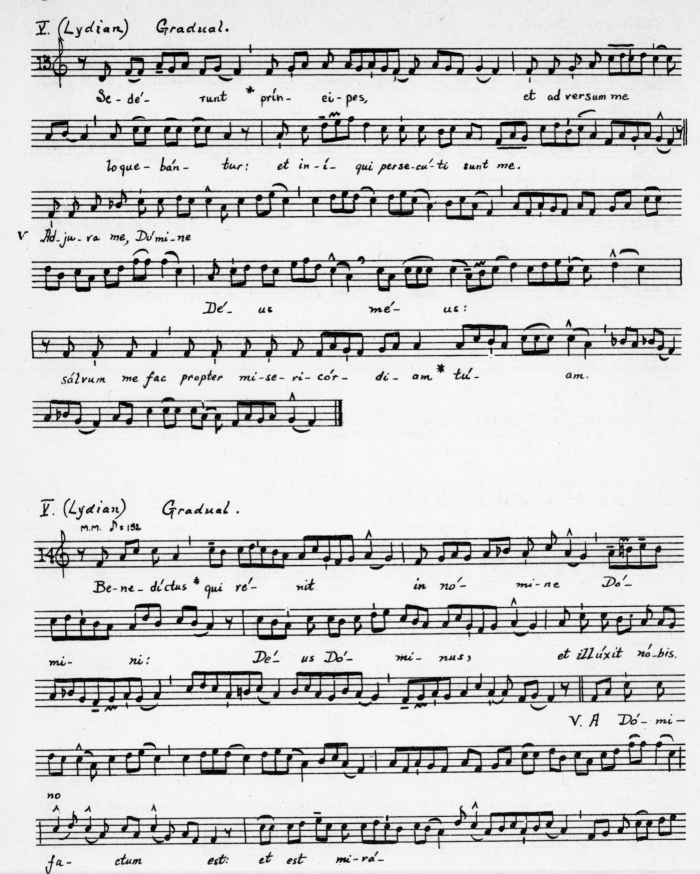

V. (Lydian) Gradual.

Se - dé - runt *prín - ci - pes,   et ad versum me

loque - bán - tur: et in - í - qui perse-cu'-ti sunt me.

V Ad-ju - ra me, Dó'mi - ne

Dé - us mé - us:

sálvum me fac propter mi-se-ri-cór-di - am*tú - am.

V. (Lydian) Gradual.

M.M. ♪ = 152

Be - ne - dí'ctus * qui ré' - nit   in no' - mi - ne Do' -

mi - ni: Dé' - us Do' - mi - nus,   et illúxit nó-bis.

V. A Dó' - mi -

no

fa - ctum   est: et est mi-rá -

bi- le * in ó- cu lis nó- stris.

VI. (Hypolydian) Communion.

M.M. ♪ = 160

Páscha nóstrum im-mo-la-tus est Christus, al-

-le-lu- ia: í-ta- que e-pu-lé- mur in á- zy-

mis sin-ce- ri-ta-tis et ve-ri- tá- tis, al-le- lú- ia, al-le-

lú- ia, al-le- lú- ia

VII. (Mixolydian) Antiphon.

M.M. ♪ = 138

XIII c.

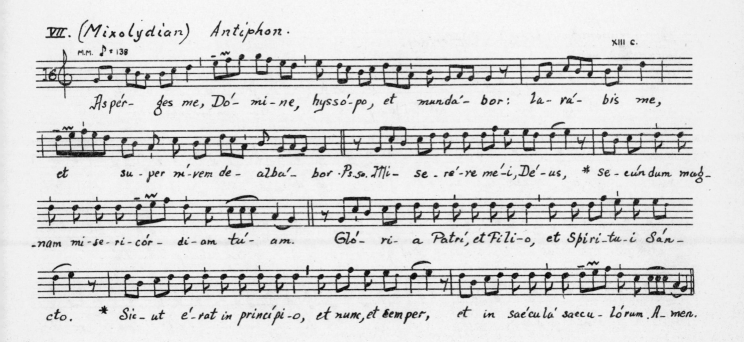

Aspér- ges me, Dó- mi-ne, hyssó-po, et mundá- bor: la-vá- bis me,

et su-per ní-vem de-albá- bor. Ps. 50. Mi- se- ré-re me-í, Dé-us, * se-cúndum mag-

-nam mi-se-ri-cór- di-am tú- am. Gló- ri- a Patrí, et Fili-o, et Spiri-tu-i Sán-

cto. * Sic-ut é-rat in princí-pi-o, et nunc,et semper, et in saécula saecu-ló-rum. A-men.

8

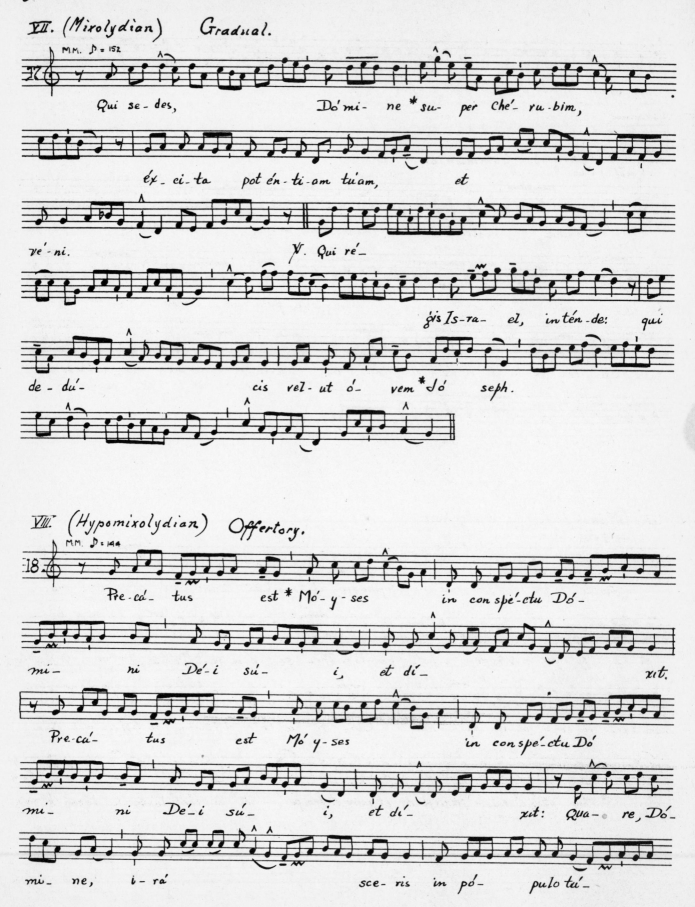

VII. (Mixolydian) Gradual.

M.M. ♪ = 152

Qui se-des, Dó-mi-ne*su-per Ché-ru-bim,

éx-ci-ta pot én-ti-am túam, et

vé-ni. ℣. Qui ré-

gis Is-ra-el, in tén-de: qui

de-dú- cis vel-ut ó- vem*Jó- seph.

VIII. (Hypomixolydian) Offertory.

M.M. ♪ = 144

Pre-cá- tus est*Mó-y-ses in con spé-ctu Dó-

mi- ni Dé-i sú- i, et dí- xit.

Pre-cá- tus est Mó-y-ses in con spé-ctu Dó

mi- ni Dé-i sú- i, et dí- xit: Qua-re, Dó-

mi- ne, i-rá sce-ris in pó- pulo tú-

o? Pár- ce í-rae á nimae tú- ae:
me mén- to Abraham, I- sa-ac et Já-cob,
quibus ju-rá-sti dá-re terram flu-én-tem lac et
mel. Et pla-cá-tus fá-ctus est Dó- mi- nus de ma-
lig ni-tá'te, quam dí- xit fá- ce- re pó-pu-lo
sú- o.

VIII. (Hypomixolydian) Introit.

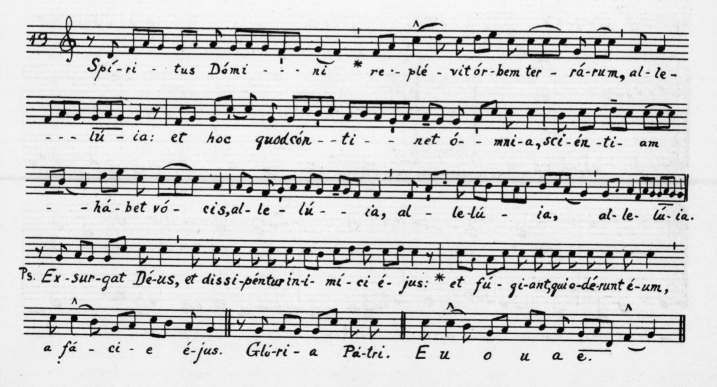

Spí-ri- tus Dómi- - -ni *re-plé-vit ór-bem ter- rá-rum, al-le-
- - -lú- ia: et hoc quod cón- -ti- net ó- mni-a, sci-én-ti- am
- -há-bet vó- cis, al-le-lú- ia, al- le-lú- ia, al-le- lú-ia.
Ps. Ex-sur-gat Dé-us, et dissi-pén tur in-i- mí-ci é- jus: * et fú- gi-ant, qui o-dé-runt é-um,
a fá- ci- e é-jus. Gló-ri-a Pá-tri. E u o u a e.

12 Cantiones duarum vocum.

Orlandus Lassus.

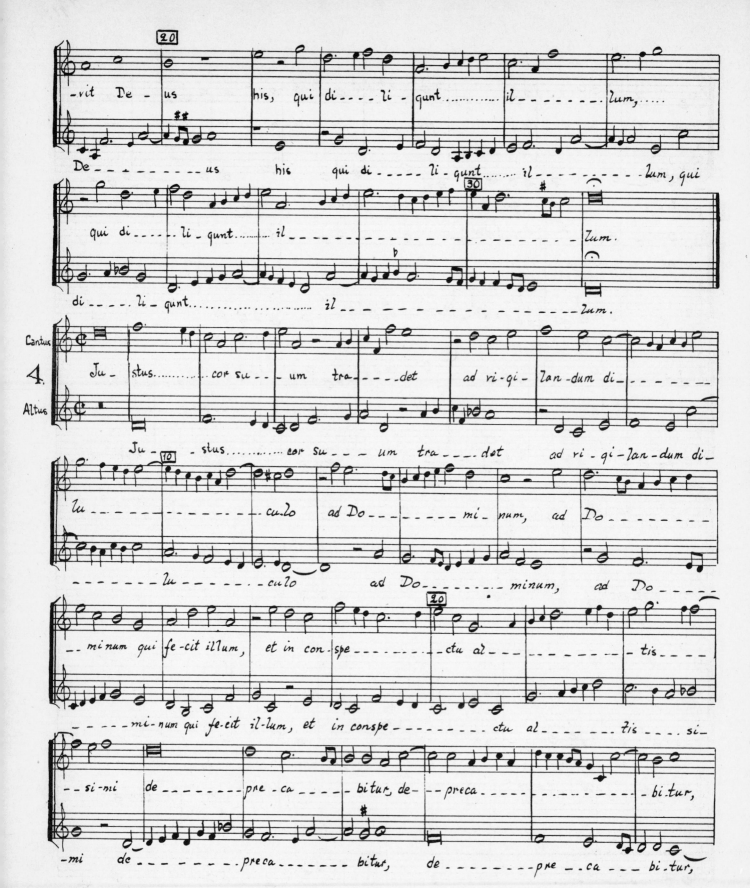

14.

Benedictus.

Orlandus Lassus.

Mass: Vestiva i Colli: Kyrie — Palestrina.

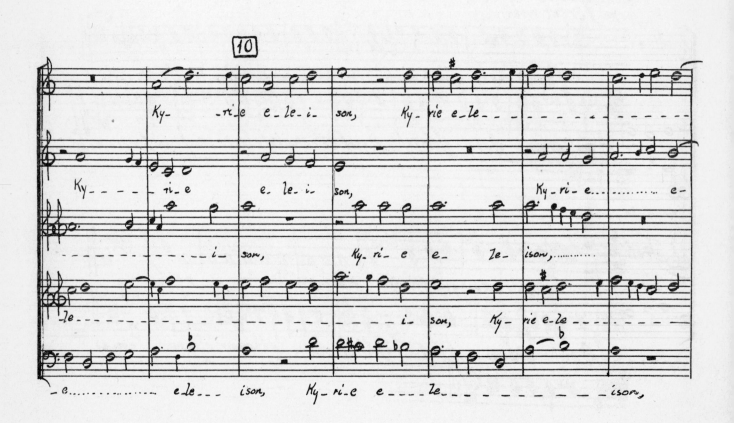

20

Mass: Vestiva i Colli: *Gloria.* *Palestrina.*

29

po_tens.............................. Do_ mine Fi.li_ u_ ni&e-ni_te,............ Je........ su

o_ mni.....po_tens. Domine Fili u-ni_&e.ni_te, Je _ su Chri___

.... Do_ mine Fi li.u_ni_&e__ni_te, Je_su Chri__ste,Je _ su

__ po_tens................... Domine Fili u__ni&e_ni_te,Je__su_ Je_ su.......

__ po_tens................................ Je _ _ _su Chri___

Chri_____ ste Fi _lius Pa _____

ste. Do_mine De_us, A___&nus De _i, Fi_lius Pa _____

Chri_____ ste......... Do_mine De_us, A&nus De_ i,

.... Chri____ste. Do_mine Deus,A&nus De _____i, Fi__li_us

__ _ _ ___ste. Domine De_us,A&nus De_____i,

90

de_ pre_ca_ti_o nem no_ stram.

_ca_ti_onem no_stram, de_preca_ti_onem no___stram. Qui se_des ad dex_

_ca_ti_onem no__stram, de_preca_ti_onem no_stram. Qui se_des ad dex__te_ram Pa_

_ca_ti_onem no_stram, de_ preca_ti_onem no__stram, Qui se_des ad dex_teram Pa_

_ca_ti_onem no_ stram. Qui sedes ad dex__teram Pa_

100

Mi_ se_re_ re no_____bis. Quo_ ni_am tu so_lus san_

te_ram Pa_tris, mi_se_re_re no_____bis. Quoni_am tu, quo_

___tris,_____ Quo_ ni_am tu so____lus san_

_tris, mi_se_re_re no_____bis_____ Quo_ni_am tu so_lus

_tris. Quoni_am tu_____solus san_

-ctus, tu so_lus Domi nus, tu solus Al_tis.si mus, Altis_si_mus, Je___

_ niam tu solus san _ _ _ _ ctus, tu solus Dominus, tu solus Al _ tis.si mus,

-ctus, san _ _ _ _ ctus, tu solus Do mi _ nus,............... tu solus Al_

san _ _ _ _ ctus, tu solus Do _ _ mi nus,...... tu solus Al_tis si mus,.......

_ _ ctus, tu solus Al _ _ tissimus, Al_tissimus,

_ _ su Chri_ste, Je_su Chri_ _ _ _ ste...... Cum sancto Spiri_tu......................

Je _ su...... Chri_ste. Cum sancto Spi _ _ _ _ _ _ _ _ _ _ _ _ _ _ ri_tu in gloria..De_

_tissimus, Je_su Christe. Cum sancto Spi_ri_tu,.......... cum sancto Spiri_tu in gloria De_i

Je _ _ _ _ _ _ su Chri_ _ _ _ _ste...... Cum san_cto Spi_ri_ tu.........

Je_ su...... Chri_ _ _ _ste. Cum sancto Spiri _tu in gloria De_i

Motet: Veni sancte Spiritus.

Palestrina.

Chorus I

Chorus II

Chorus I

Chorus II

Chorus I

Chorus II

39.

Chorus I.

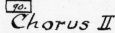

Chorus II

Chorus I

Chorus I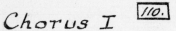

Chorus II

120.

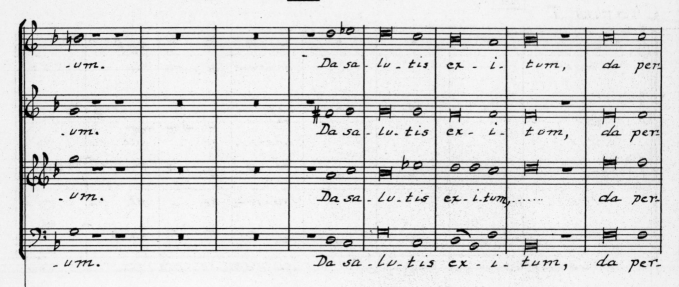

.um. Da sa‐lu‐tis ex‐i‐tum, da per‐

.um. Da sa‐lu‐tis ex‐i‐tum, da per‐

.um. Da sa‐lu‐tis ex‐i‐tum,....... da per‐

.um. Da sa‐lu‐tis ex‐i‐tum, da per‐

Da vir‐tu‐tis me‐ri‐tum, da per‐

Da vir‐tu‐tis me‐ri‐tum, da per‐

.um.Da vir‐tu‐tis me‐ri‐tum, da per‐

Da vir‐tu‐tis me‐ri‐tum, da per‐

Mass: Sine Nomine: Sanctus. Palestrina.

Mass: De Feria: Kyrie.   Palestrina.

Mass: Sanctorum Meritis: Agnus Dei I and II.   Palestrina.

Hymn: In Festo Transfigurationis Domini.

Palestrina.

Mass: Repleatur os meum laude.

Palestrina

64.

Sanctus

Hosanna

Benedictus

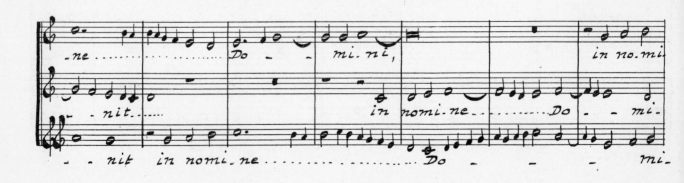

71.

Hosanna ut supra.

Agnus Dei. I.

Agnus Dei. II

Magnificat.

Gregorian: 1.

Palestrina.

Gregorian: 3.

78.

Gregorian: 9.

Carl Fischer, Inc. New York.
No. 4 -12 lines.

Gregorian: 11.

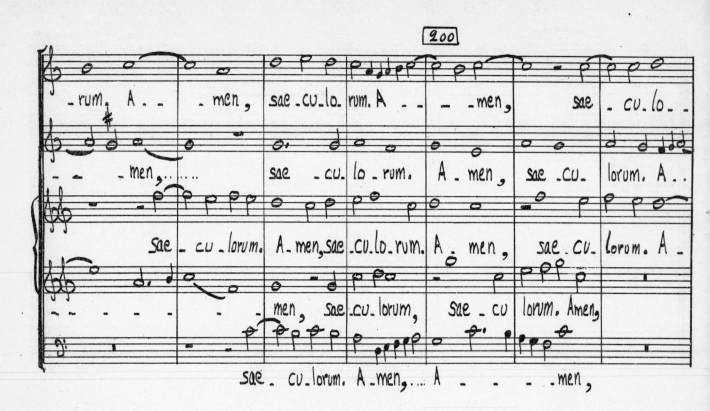

Mass: Ad Fugam: Kyrie. Palestrina.

20

Mass: Ad Fugam: Hosanna.

Palestrina.

Trinitas in unitate.

Mass: Ad Fugam: Benedictus.

Palestrina.

Mass: Ad Fugam: Agnus Dei. Palestrina.

92.

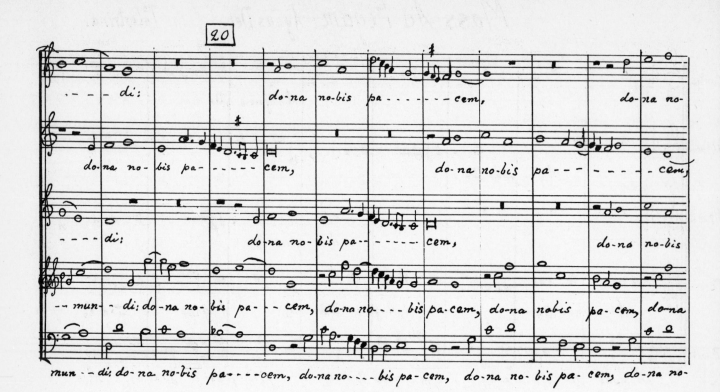

Mass: L. homme armé

Kyrie

Palestrina.

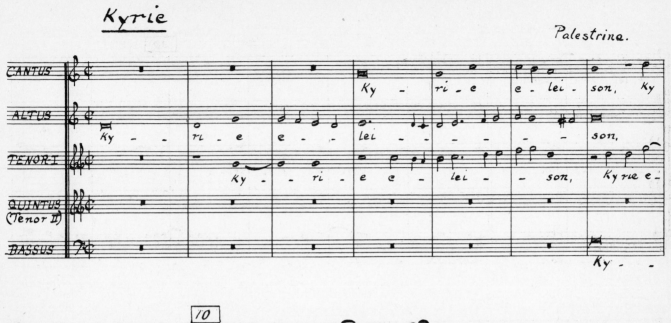

96.

70

Gloria in excelsis Deo.

130

.ste, Je _ su Chri _ ste. Cum sancto Spi.ri tu, cum sancto Spi _ ri _ tu

.ste, Je _ su Chri _ ste. Cum sancto Spi.ri tu, cum sancto Spi _ ri _ tu

.... Je _ su Chri _ ste. Cum sancto Spiri tu, cum sancto Spiri _ tu in glo _

.su Chri _ _ ste. De _ _

.ste, Je _ su Chri _ ste. Cum sancto Spiri tu......... in

140

in glo _ ria De _ i Pa _ _ .tris............. A _ men.

.... in glo.ri a De _ i Pa.tris.A _ _ _ men.

.ri.a De _ _ _ i Pa _ _ _ .tris A _ _ men.

.i Pa _ tris. A _ men.

glo _ ri.a De _ i Pa_tris............. A _ men A _ men.

Credo in unum Deum.

CANTUS

Pa.trem o _ mni. po _

ALTUS

Pa-trem o _ mni.po _ ten _ _ _ tem,.............

TENOR I

Pa- trem o _ mni-po.ten _ _ _

QUINTUS (Tenor II)

BASSUS

Pa trem o.mni po.ten _ _ _ _ _ tem, omni po.ten.tem,

104.

80

90

100

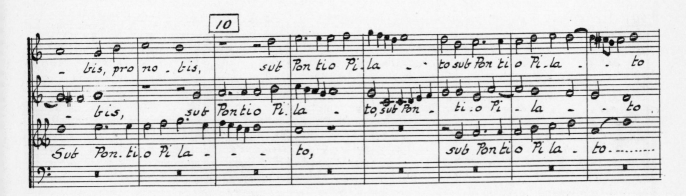

Sanctus

30

40

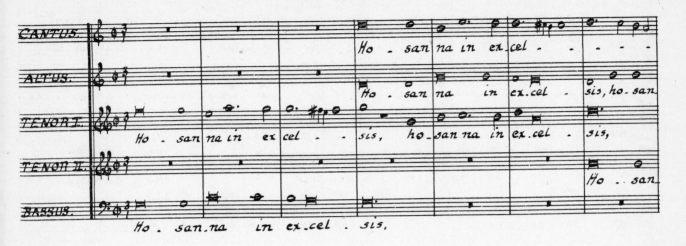

Benedictus

Agnus Dei. I

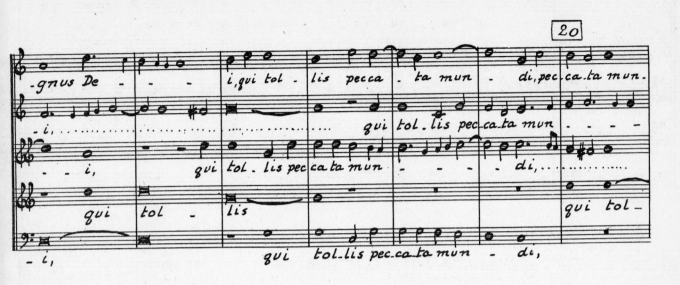

Agnus Dei. II.

Motet : Laudate Dominum in tympanis

Palestrina.

124.

hymnum cante - mus Do - mi.no, De.o
hymnum cante - mus Do - mi no, De.o
hymnumcante - mus Do - mi no, De.o
hymnumcante - mus Do - mi no, De.o
I
Hymnumcante - - mus Do - mi.no,
Hymnum cante - mus Do - mi.no,
Hymnumcante - mus Do - mi.no,
Hymnumcante - mus Do - mi.no,
II
.numcante - mus hymnumcante - - mus Do - mi.no, De - .o no - stro
numcante - mus hymnumcante - mus Do - mi no, ... De - o no - stro
numcante - mus hymnum can. te - mus Do - mi no Do - mi.no, Deo no - stro
numcante - mus hymnum cante - - mus Do - mi.no, De - o no.stro

Motet: O admirabile commercium

Palestrina.

132

135.

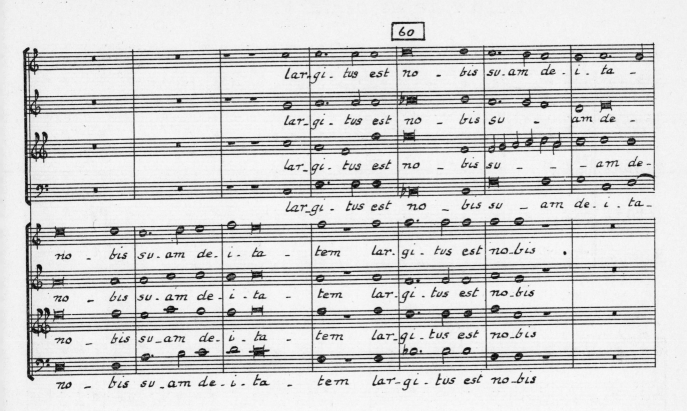

Litaniae de Beata Virgine Maria.

Palestrina.

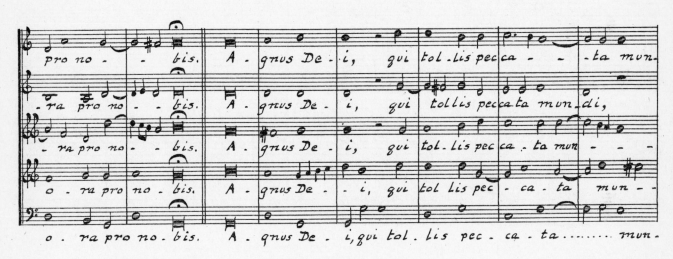

Motet: Dies Sanctificatus.

Palestrina.

Mass: Dies Sanctificatus: Kyrie. Palestrina.

Motet: Alleluia Tulerunt.

Palestrina.

150.

Hymn: In Dominicis Quadragesima.

Palestrina.

Hymn: In Dominicis Qudragesima.

Palestrina.

Mass: Petra Sancta: Kyrie. Palestrina.

Mass: Gabriel Archangelus: Hosanna. Palestrina.

Mass: Gabriel Archangelus: Benedictus.

Palestrina.

Offertory: Laudate Dominum.

Palestrina.

40

Offertory: Improperium. *Palestrina.*

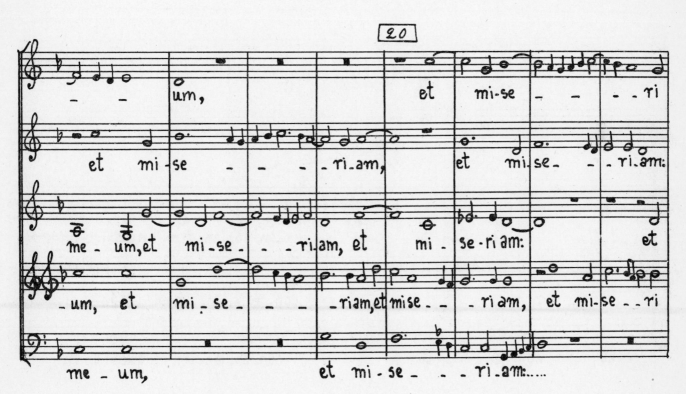

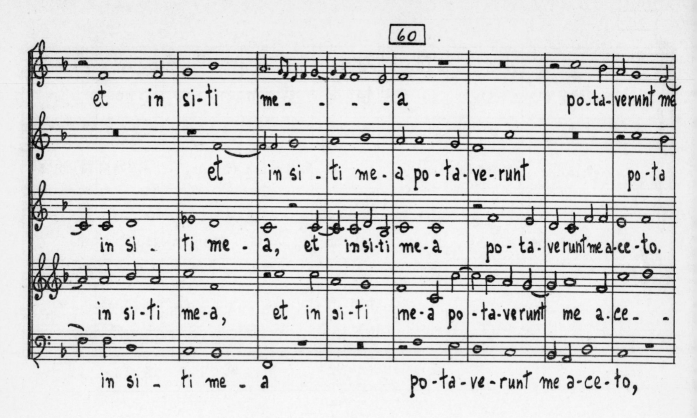

Offertory: Exaltabo Te. *Palestrina.*

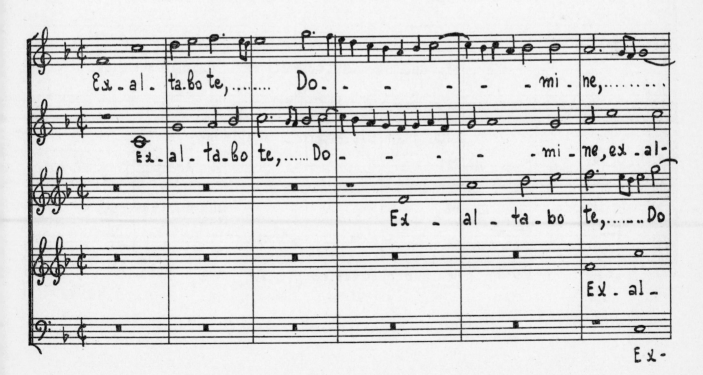

40

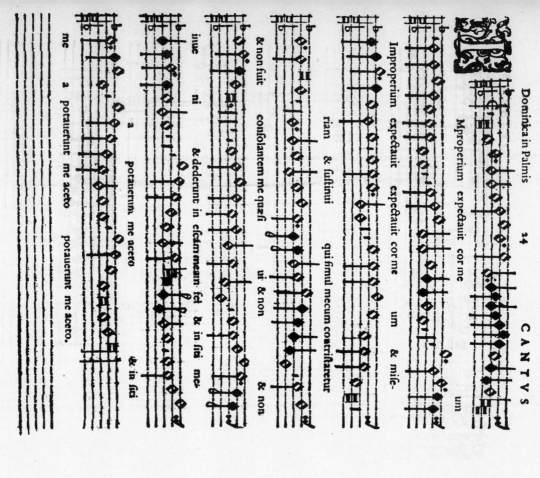

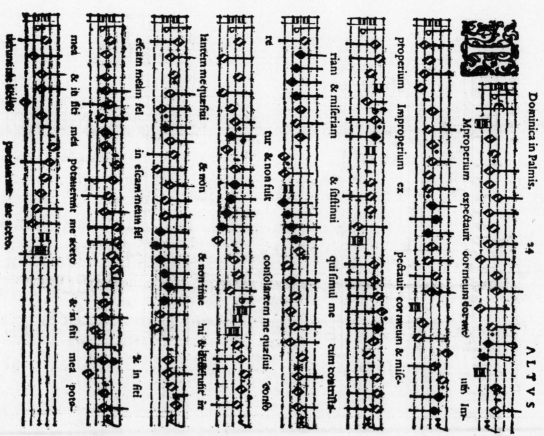

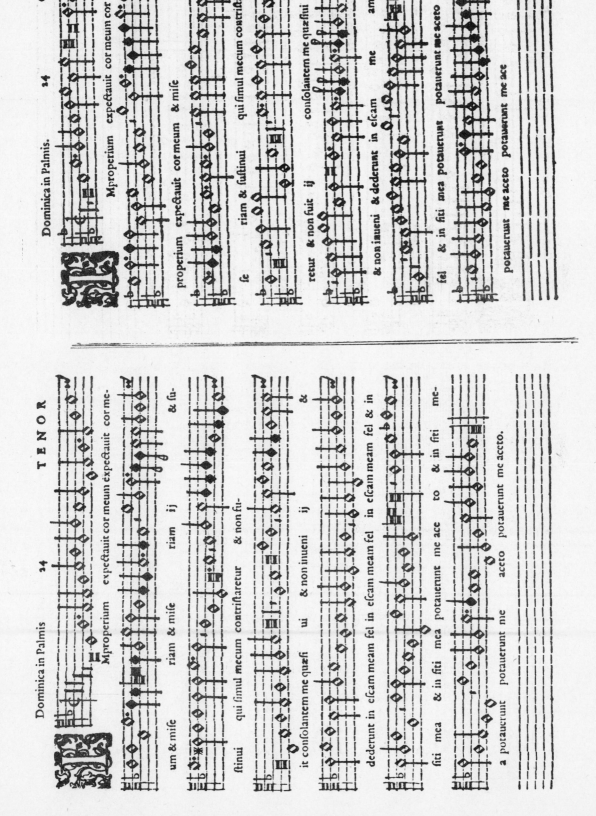

184

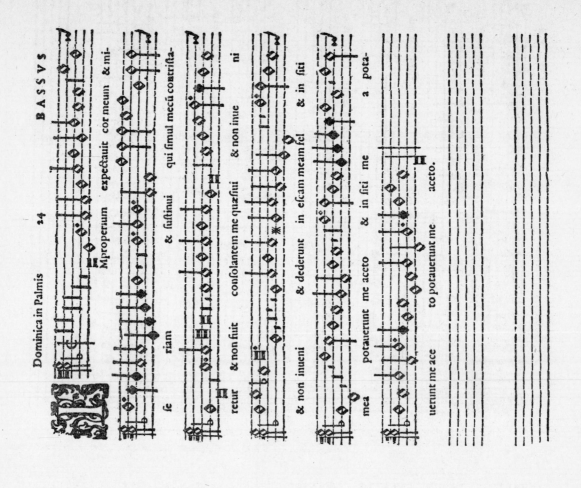

Mass: Ut Re Mi Fa Sol La: Kyrie

Palestrina

Gloria in excelsis Deo

De - i, Fi - li - us........ Pa-tris, Filius Pa _ tris.

Fi-li-us........ Pa-tris, Fi-li-us........ Pa _ tris.

De - i, Filius Pa _ tris, Filius Pa-tris, Fi-li-us........ Pa _ tris.

_ _ i, Filius Pa-tris, Filius Pa _ tris.

Fili-us Pa _ _ tris, Fi-li-us........ Pa _ tris.

De _ i, Fi - lius Pa-tris, Fili-us Pa _ tris.

Qui tollis pec-cata mun-di, mi-se-re-re no _ bis, mi-

Qui tollis pec-cata mun-di, mi-se-re-re no _ bis,

Qui tollis pec-ca _ ta mun-di, mi-se-re-re no _ bis,

Qui tol-lis peccata mun _ di, mi-se-re-re no _ bis,

Qui tollis pec-ca........mun _ di, mi-se-rere no _ bis,

Qui tollis pecca-ta mun-di, mi-se-re-re no _ bis,

_ _ se-re-re no _ bis. Qui tol-lis pec-cata mun _ di,

mi-se-re-re no _ bis. Qui tol-lis peccata mun _ di,

mi-se-re-re no _ bis. Qui tol-lis peccata mun _ di,

mi-se-rere........no-bis. Qui tol-lis pec-ca-ta mun _ di,

mi _ se-re-re no _ bis. Qui tol-lis pec-ca-ta mun _ di,

mi-se-re-re no _ bis.

Credo in unum Deum.

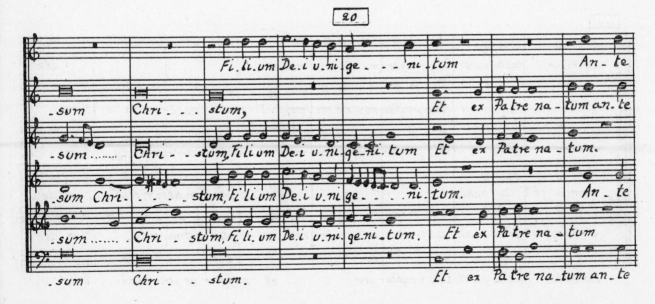

o - mnia........saecu...la. De_um de De__o, lu mer de lu mi_ne, De __um ve_rum de

o _ mnia sae_cu la. Lu_men de lu mi ne, De _ um ve_rum de

De um de De __o, lu men de lu mi ne, De _ um verum de

o _ mnia sae_cu la. De um de De_o, lu men de lu mi ne, De _ um verum de

De _ um de De o, lu men de Lu mine De _ um............ ve _ rum

o _ mnia sae_cu la. Lu men de lumi ne, De _ um ve_rum de

De __ o ve ___ ro. Ge nitum non fa_ctum consubstanti a _ lem Pa _ tri: per quem

De _ o ve _ ro. Consubstanti a _ lem Pa _ tri.

De __ o ve __ ro. Ge nitum non factum con_substanti alem Pa tri.

De _ o ve _ ro. Ge ni tum non fa _ ctum: per quem

de De_o ve _ ro. Ge_nitum non fa_ctum, con sub stanti a lem Pa _ tri per quem

De _ o ve _ ro. consubstanti a _ lem Pa _ tri per quem

omni a facta sunt. Qui propter nos, homi _ nes, de_

Qui propter nos, ho mi _ nes, et propter no stram sa lu _ tem

Qui propter nos, ho mi _ nes, et propter no-stram sa tu _ tem de _

omni a fa_cta sunt. Et propter na stram salu _ tem de_

omni a facta sunt. Qui propter nos, homi nes, et propter nostram salu _ tem de

omni a facta sunt. Qui propter nos, et propter no-stram salu _ tem

50

60

70

198.

200.

Sanctus

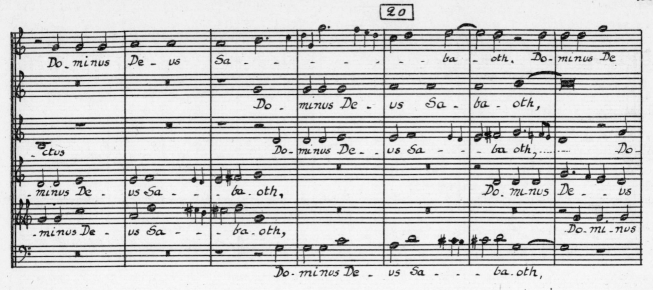

206.

Agnus Dei I

210.

214.

16 _ Response.

Ingegneri.

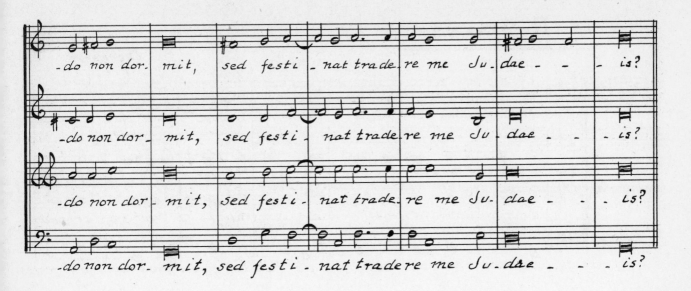

-do non dor - mit, sed festi - nat trade - re me Judae - - - is?

-do non dor - mit, sed festi - nat trade - re me Judae - - - is?

-do non dor - mit, sed festi - nat trade - re me Judae - - - is?

-do non dor - mit, sed festi - nat tradere me Judae - - - is?

30

CANTUS I — V. Quid dor - mi - tis? sur - gi - te, et o - ra -

CANTUS II — V. Quid dor - mi - tis? sur - gi - te, et o - ra - - -

ALTUS — V. Quid dor - mi - tis? sur - gi - te, et o - ra -

-te, ne intre - tis in ten - ta - ti - o - - nem.

"Vel Judam"
ut supra

-te, ne in - tre - tis in ten - ta - ti - o - - nem.

-te ne in - tre - tis in tentati - o - - nem.

216.

18 Response.

Ingegneri.

CANTUS — Omnes ami-ci me-i de-re lique-runt me, et prae-

ALTUS — Omnes ami-ci me-i de-relique-runt me, et prae-

TENOR — Omnes ami-ci me-i de-relique-runt me, et prae-

BASSUS — Omnes ami-ci me-i de-re-li-que-runt me, et prae-

10

-valu-e-runt insi-di-an-tes mi-hi: tra-didit me quem di-

-valu-e-runt insi-di-an-tes mi-hi: tra-didit me quem di-

-valu-e-runt insi-di-an-tes mi-hi: tra-didit me quem di-

valu-e-runt insi-di-an-tes mi-hi: tra-didit me quem di-

20

-li-ge-bam: Et ter-ri-bi-li-bus o-cu-lis pla-ga cru-

-li-ge-bam: Et ter-ri-bi-li-bus o-cu-lis pla-ga cru-

-li-ge-bam: Et ter-ri-bi-li-bus o-cu-lis pla-ga cru-

-li-ge-bam: Et ter-ri-bi-li-bus o-cu-lis pla-ga cru-

_de_ _ li per cu tien tes a ce to po ta bant me.

30

CANTUS I V. In ter in i quos pro je ce runt me et non

CANTUS II V. Et non

ALTUS V. Inter in i quos pro je cerunt me et non

peperce runt a nimae, a nimae me ae.

„Et terribilibus" ut supra

peperce runt a nimae me ae.

peperce runt a nimae me ae.

21. Responsé.

Ingegneri.

Tam — — quam ad la.tro.nem ex.i.stis cum gla.di.is et fus.ti.

Tam — — quam ad la.tro — nem ex.i.stis cum gla.di.is et fusti.

Tam — quam ad la.tro — nem ex.i.stis cum gla.di.is et fusti.

Tam — quam ad la.tro.nem ex.i.stis cum gla.di.is et fusti.

.bus com.pre.hen.de.re . . . . . me: Quo.ti.di.e a.pud

.bus com.pre.hen.de.re me: Quo.ti.di.e a.

.bus com.pre.hen.de.re me: Quo.ti.di.e a.

.bus com.pre.hen.de.re me: Quo.ti.di.e a.

vos e.ram in tem.plo do.cens et non me te.nu.i.stis:et ec.ce

.pud vos e.ram in tem.plo do.cens et non me te.nu.i.stis: et

.pud vos e.ram in tem.plo do.cens et non me te.nu.i.stis:

.pud vos e.ram in tem.plo do.cens et non me te.nu.i.stis:et ec.ce

flagel la — tum du.ci.tis ad cru.ci.fi — .dum.

ecce flagel.la.tum du.ci.tis ad cru.ci.fi gen — .dum.

du.ci.tis ad cru.ci.fi gen — .dum.

flagel la — tum du.ci.tis ad cru.ci.fi gen — .dum.

22 Response.
Ingegneri.

ce ma-gna: De-us me- - us, ut quid me de-re-li-qui- -sti?

Et in-cli- -na-to ca- -pi-te e-mi-sit spi - ri - tum.

CANTUS I
V. Ex-cla-mans Je-sus vo-ce ma- -gna, a-

CANTUS II
V. Ex-cla-mans Je-sus voce ma- -gna, voce ma- -gna, a-

ALTUS
V. Ex-cla-mans Je-sus voce ma- gna, a-

-it: Pa-ter in manus tu-as commendo spi-ri-tum me-um.

-it: Pa-ter in manus tu-as commen-do spi-ri-tum me- -um.

"Et inclinato" ut supra

-it Pa-ter in manus tu-as commen-do spi-ri-tum me- um.

221.

23. Response.   Ingegneri.

-ces adver.sa.ri.us, di.cens Con.gre.ga.mini, et prope.ra - - te ad devoran.

-ces adver.sa.ri.us di.cens Con.gre.ga.mi.ni et. pro.pe.rate ad devoran.

.ces ad ver.sa.ri.us di.cens Con.gre ga.mini, et prope.ra - te ad

.ces ad ver.sa.ri.us di.cens: Con.gre ga mini, et prope.ra - te ad devo.

30

..dum il - - lum: po.su.erunt me in deser -to so.li.tu.di.

dum ad devorandum il - lum: po.su.erunt me in deser.to so.li.tu.di.

de vorandum il - lum: po.su.erunt me in deser.to so.li.tu.di.

.randum il - lum: po.su.erunt me in deser.to so.li.tu.di.

40

.nis et luxit super me o.mnis ter - - ra: Qui.a non

.nis et luxit super me o.mnis ter - ra:

.nis et luxit super me o.mnis ter - - ra: Qui.a non est in.ven -

.nis et luxit super me o.mnis ter _ _ ra: Qui.a non

est in ven_tus qui me a _ gno _ sce _ ret,..... et fa _ cer _ et be _ ne.

Qui_a non est in ven_ tus qui me a_gno_sce_ret, et fa _ ceret be _ _ ne.

tus qui me a_gno_sce_ret, qui me a_gnosce_ret, et fa_ce_ret be _ ne.

est in_ven_tus qui me a _ gno _ sce_ret, et fa _ ce_ret be _ ne.

CANTUS I — V. In_surre_xe_runt in me vi_ri abs_que mise_ri_cor_di_a,

CANTUS II — V. In_surre_xe runt in me vi_ri abs_que mi_se_ri cordia,

ALTUS — V. In_surre_xe_runt in me vi_ri abs_que misericor_di_a,

et non peper_ce_runt a_ni_mae me _ _ ae.

et non peper_ce_runt a_nimae me _ _ ae.

et non peper_ce_runt a_nimae me _ _ ae.

„Quia" ut supra
„Animam meam"
ibidem usque ad V

32. Response.

Ingegneri.

Et e_rit in pa_ce me_mo_ri_a e_jus.

Et e_rit in pa_ce me_mo_ri_a e_jus.

Et e_rit in pa_ce me_mo_ri_a e_jus.

Et e_rit in pa_ce me_mo_ri_a e_jus.

30

CANTUS I — V. Tam_quam a_gnus co_ram ton_dente se

CANTUS II — V. Tam_quam a_gnus co_ram ton_dente se ob_mu_tu_it, co_ram ton_dente

ALTUS — V. Tam_quam a_gnus co_ram ton_dente se ob_mu_tu_it,

40

ob_mu_tu_it, et non a_pe_ru_it os su_um: de an_gu_sti_

se ob_mu_tu_it, et non a_pe_ru_it os su_um: de an_

et non a_pe_ru_it os su_um: de an_gu_sti_

_a, et de ju_di_ci_o sub_la_tus est, sub_la_tus est. „Et erit" ut supra

_gu_sti_a, et de ju_di_ci_o sub_la_tus est sub_la_tus est. Ecce quomodo ut supra usque ad V.

_a et de ju_di_ci_o sub_la_tus est, sub_la_tus est.

MOTET: IN FESTO APOSTOLORUM.

MASS: O REGEM COELI : HOSANNA

PALESTRINA.

GREGORIAN CHANT

Gregorian chant, or plain song, is the name of unisonous ecclesiastical art music in use in the Christian Church of the West before the development of harmony, written on scales derived from the Greek modes.

The modes used in plain song were limited, quite early, to four authentic, (Dorian, Phrygian, Lydian, and Mixolydian), and four plagal (Hypodorian, Hypophrygian, Hypolydian, and Hypomixolydian) modes.

This modal system is different from that of the original Greek modes, due to some misunderstanding of the latter.

There are two main collections of Gregorian chant: the Gradual* and the Antiphonal. In the Gradual the chief ancient pieces are: the Introit, or Antiphona ad introitum, at the beginning of the service; the Gradual, with Alleluia or tract, which precede the Gospel; the Offertory which accompanies the preparation of the oblations; the Communion or antiphona ad Communionem which accompanies the partaking of the Sacrament.

In the parallel collection of music, the Antiphonal, we find the Responds which form musical interludes between the lessons and the Antiphons which form an integral part of the Psalmody. This collection is used mainly in the monasteries for the singing of the Office.

In both collections the modes are indicated by the numbers one to eight.

————————————————

*The most important parts of the Gradual and Antiphonal are available in modern notation (Liber Usualis).

The relation of plain song to measured music may be expressed thus: plain song is analogous to prose, and measured music, with its definite, generally regular, subdivisions of time, is analogous to poetry, with its definite subdivisions of metre.

Explanation of signs found in Gregorian chant:

 Ictus. The rhythmical ictus is an alighting or resting place sought by the rhythm at intervals of every two or three (eighth) notes. It does not mean accent or stress. The rhythm is of the simplest, i.e., two or three eighth notes, their order of succession free.

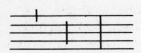 Musical punctuation, in general corresponding to comma, semicolon, period.

∧ Pressus, a neum meaning a compact strong sound of double value, demanding, in many cases, some degree of acceleration on the preceding notes.

Distropha and tristropha, meaning a twice or thrice repeated vocal pulsation, very rapid in character, like a hand tapping (according to ancient authority).

V. Verse (from the psalms).

℞ Back to response.

i ii iij 1, ii repeated; iij to be sung three times.

―― Episema, meaning holding.

e u o u a e Saeculorum Amen (end of Gloria Patri).

Asterisk meaning division of the choir according to previous agreement.

 Quilisma. The note or the group of notes immediately preceding the note below or above this sign must be prolonged. It appeared in the old notation as a jagged neume.

The above signs are all taken from the modern notation in Liber Usualis.

13. Gradual. The mode is mixed, i.e., it has both b and b flat. With   6
modulation.
Princes sat, and spoke against me: and the wicked persecuted me: help
me, O Lord, my God: Save me for thy mercy's sake.

14. Gradual. Benedictus. In the Lydian mode (mixed).   6

15. Communion.   Recorded by the Solesmes Monks.   7
Christ our Pasch is immolated, alleluia: therefore let us feast with the
unleavened bread of sincerity and truth. Alleluia, alleluia, alleluia.

16. Antiphon.   7
Thou shalt sprinkle me with hyssop, O Lord, and I shall be cleansed; thou
shalt wash me, and I shall be made whiter than snow. Ps. 50. Have mercy
on me, O God, according to thy great mercy. V. Glory be to the Father,
and to the Son, and to the Holy Ghost. As it was in the beginning, is
now, and ever shall be, world without end. Amen.

17. Gradual.   Recorded by the Solesmes Monks.   8
Thou, O Lord, that sittest upon the Cherubim, stir up thy might, and
come. V. Give ear, O thou that rulest Israel: thou that leadest Joseph
like a sheep.

18. Offertory.   Recorded by the Solesmes Monks.   8
Moses prayed in the sight of the Lord his God, and said: Why, O Lord, is
thy indignation enkindled against thy people, Let the anger of thy mind
cease; remember Abraham, Isaac, and Jacob, to whom thou didst swear to
give a land flowing with milk and honey: and the Lord was appeased from
doing the evil, which he had spoken of doing against his people.

19. Introit.   Recorded by the Solesmes Monks.   9
The Spirit of the Lord hath filled the whole earth, alleluia; and that
which containeth all things hath knowledge of the voice, alleluia, alleluia, alleluia. Ps. 67. Let God arise, and let his enemies be scattered; and let them that hate him, flee from before his face. V. Glory.

Orlandus Lassus (1532-94).

Cantiones duarum vocum. In all the modes used in ecclesiastical style.
Texts from the Vulgate: 10

1. Eccl. 14:22.
Blessed is the man that shall continue in wisdom, and that shall medi-
tate in his justice, and in his mind shall think of the all seeing eye
of God.

                                                                          10
2. Proverbs 3: 13,14.
Blessed is the man that findeth wisdom and is rich in prudence: The pur-
chasing thereof is better than the merchandize of silver, and her fruit
than the chiefest and purest gold.

                                                                          11
3. I Cor. 2:9.
That eye hath not seen, nor ear heard, neither hath it entered into the
heart of man, what things God hath prepared for them that love God.

4. Eccl. 39:6.
   He will give his heart to resort early to the Lord that made him, and he
   will pray in the sight of the most high.

5. Proverbs 10: 28,29.
   The expectation of the just is joy; but the hope of the wicked shall per-
   ish. The strength of the upright is the way of the Lord: and fear to
   them that work evil.

6. John 8:12.
   He that followeth me, walketh not in darkness but shall have the light of
   life, sayeth the Lord.

7. Book of Wisdom 10:19.
   The just took the spoils of the wicked, and they sung to thy holy name,
   O Lord, and they praised with one accord thy victorious hand.

8. This is part of the responsory for Lesson VI in Matins for the Feast of
   All Saints, Nov. 1.
   My holy people, who in this world have known only toil and strife, I
   shall grant to you the reward for all your labors.

9. Matthew 16:24.
   If any man will come after me, let him deny himself, and take up his
   cross, and follow me, sayeth the Lord.

10. Matthew 25:23.
    Well done, good and faithful servant: because thou hast been faithful
    over a few things I will place thee over many things: enter thou into
    the joy of thy Lord.

11. Book of Wisdom 3:7. Matt. 13:43.
    The just shall shine, and shall run to and fro like sparks among the
    reeds.

12. Motet in honor of the Blessed Virgin Mary.
    As a rose among thorns even to them its beauty lends,
    So the Virgin Mary casts her grace and charm
    Over all her progeny.   For from her has sprung
    The Flower, whose fragrance is the gift of life.

Giovanni Pierluigi Palestrina (1525-94)
His liturgical compositions include ninety-three masses (thirty-nine in four,
twenty-nine in five, twenty-one in six and four in eight parts; one hundred and
thirty-nine motets in four to twelve parts; Lamentations, Offertories, Magnificats, Litanies, Hymns, and Vesper psalms. The thematic material was drawn from
Gregorian chant as well as madrigals, motets and secular music, according to the
custom of the time.

Translation of the text of the Mass:
Kyrie eleison, Christe eleison, Kyrie eleison.
Lord, have mercy. Christ, have mercy. Lord, have mercy.

Gloria: Glory be to God on high (intoned by the priest).
Choir: And on earth peace to men of good will. We praise thee; we bless thee;
we adore thee; we glorify thee. We give thee thanks for thy great glory, O Lord,
heavenly King. God the Father Almighty. O Lord Jesus Christ, the only-begotten
Son: O Lord God, Lamb of God, Son of the Father, who taketh away the sins of the
world, have mercy on us: who taketh away the sins of the world, receive our
prayers: who sitteth at the right hand of the Father, have mercy on us. For
thou only art holy: thou only art Lord: thou only, O Jesus Christ, are most
high, together with the Holy Ghost, in the glory of God the Father, Amen.

Credo: I believe in one God (intoned by the priest).
Choir: The Father Almighty, maker of heaven and earth, and of all things visible
and invisible. And in one Lord Jesus Christ, the only begotten Son of God, born
of the Father before all ages; God of God, light of light, true God of true God;
begotten not made; consubstantial with the Father; by whom all things were made.
Who for us men, and for our salvation, came down from heaven; and was incarnate by
the Holy Ghost, of the Virgin Mary; and was made man. He was crucified also for
us, suffered under Pontius Pilate, and was buried. And the third day he rose
again according to the scriptures; and ascended into heaven. He sitteth at the
right hand of the Father; and he shall come again with glory to judge the living
and the dead; and his kingdom shall have no end, and in the Holy Ghost, the Lord
and giver of life, who proceedeth from the Father and the Son, who together with
the Father and the Son is adored and glorified; who spoke by the prophets. And
one holy catholic and apostolic church. I confess one baptism for the remission
of sins. And I await the resurrection of the dead, and the life of the world to
come. Amen.

Sanctus: Holy, holy, holy, Lord God of hosts. Heaven and earth are full of thy
glory. Hosanna in the highest.
Benedictus: Blessed is he that cometh in the name of the Lord.

Agnus Dei I: Lamb of God, who takest away the sins of the world, have mercy on
us.
Agnus Dei II: Lamb of God, who takest away the sins of the world, grant us peace.

        In the Mixolydian mode. L'Homme Armé, an old French Chan-
son used as canto fermo by a number of 15th and 16th century
masters in the composition of a mass called Missa L'Homme
Armé, the purpose of which was to show their skill and in-
genuity in the use of contrapuntal devices.

    The above theme while not fully agreeing with the canti
fermi used by the composers previous to Palestrina, may
be accepted as the standard form. It is the version re-
sulting from joining the phrases as they appear in the
mass by Palestrina.
      There are two editions of this mass: 1570 and 1599;
the first, in triple time, and the second, in $\frac{4}{2}$ time. The
curious fact about these two editions is that by changing
the triple time of the first edition to $\frac{4}{2}$ time by rebar-
ring it the result will be that of the 1599 edition with
every important cadence correctly placed.

        In the Phrygian mode. A great example of the canonic art,
in all possible intervals. (The Gloria, in canon at the
fourth, and the Credo, in canon at the fifth, are omitted
in this book, since there are numerous other examples of
imitation in these intervals.)

        In the Phrygian mode. On the Gregorian Hymn of the same
name (see Liber usualis, p. 963).

Page

Ut Re Mi Fa Sol La.   185
            In the Ionian mode. Also called the Hexachord Mass. Two
            forms of the Guidonian hexachord are used; on C (hexachor-
            dum naturale), and on G (hexachordum durum). The hexachord
            on F (hexachordum molle) is not used on account of its mod-
            ulating properties.

Vestiva i Colli   22
            In the Dorian mode. On his own madrigal of the same name.
tets:
   Alleluia Tulerunt Dominum   147
            In the Mixolydian mode.
            They have taken away my Lord, and I know not where they
            have laid him. If thou hast taken him away, tell me and I
            will take him away. (Mary Magdalen, following the resurrec-
            tion.)
            Taken from John 20:13,15 (last portion of each verse)

Dies Sanctificatus   140
            In the Mixolydian mode. A Christmas motet.
            The sacred day has dawned upon us,
            Come ye people and praise God,
            Because this day a great light has fallen upon the earth.
            (Psalm 117:24): This is the day that the Lord hath made -
            let us rejoice and be glad in it.

In Festo Apostolorum: Tollite jugum   226
In the Dorian mode

Take My yoke upon you, saith the Lord, and

learn of Me, because I am meek, and humble of

heart: For My yoke is sweet, and My burden light.

Laudate Dominum in Tympanis   123
            In the Mixolydian mode.
            Praise ye the Lord with timbrels,
            Sing ye unto the Lord with cymbals,
            Sing unto him a new song!
            Exalt him and call upon his name!
            For great and glorious is the Lord in his power,
            The Lord who putteth an end to wars.
            Sing a hymn to the Lord our God!
            (From Judith XVI - 2,16,3,15.)

O Admirabile Commercium   131
            O wondrous exchange! The Creator of mankind,
            taking upon himself a human body, has deigned
            to be born of a virgin; and thus becoming man,
            albeit without seed, he had made us sharers in
            his divinity!
            ("Commercium" literally translated means "exchange" not a
            very poetic word, but there is no other word that will as
            adequately express the dominant idea of the text, viz.,
            God taking to himself humanity, and in return bestowing
            upon humanity his divinity.)

Veni Sancte Spiritus . . . .

In the Dorian mode. An excellent example of homophonic
style.

Holy Spirit, come and shine
On our souls with beams divine
Issuing from Thy radiance bright.
Come, O Father of the poor,
Ever bounteous of Thy store.
Come our hearts' unfailing light.

Come, Consoler, kindest, best,
Come, our bosom's dearest guest,
Sweet refreshment, sweet repose.
Rest in labor, coolness sweet,
Tempering the burning heat,
Truest comfort of our woes.

O, divinest light impart,
Unto every faithful heart
Plenteous streams from love's bright flood.
But for Thy blest Deity,
Nothing pure in man could be,
Nothing harmless, nothing good.

Work away each sinful stain;
Gently shed Thy gracious rain
On the dry and fruitless soul.
Heal each wound and bend each will,
Warm our hearts benumbed and chill,
All our wayward steps control.

Note all Thy faithful just,
Who in Thee confide and trust,
Deign the sevenfold gift to send.
Grant us virtue's blest increase
Grant a death of hope and peace,
Grant the joys that never end.
(Mediaeval poem attributed to Pope Innocent III, (1161-1216).)
Translation by Father Edward Caswall.

Hymns:

In Dominicis Quadragesima: Vesper hymn on the Gregorian theme . .
"Ad preces nostras." Only the two last movements are used in
this book.
In the Aeolian mode. In the last movement the soprano and the second tenor form a canon at the octave.
Grant to us a fountain of tears, the potent strength that comes
from fasting; destroy with thy might (literally "sword") our
thousand carnal vices.
Glory be to God, the Father Eternal, and to thee, eternally begotten Son, with whom the Holy Spirit, (in all things) equal,
reigneth forever.

In Festo Transfigurationes Domini: On the Gregorian hymn . . . .
Quicumque Christum Quaeritis (see Liber Usualis, page 1465.)
In the Phrygian mode.

All ye who would the Christ descry,
Lift up your eyes to Him on high:
There mortal gaze hath strength to see
The token of His majesty.

A wondrous sign we here behold,
That knows not death nor groweth old,
Sublime, most high, that cannot fade,
That was ere earth and heaven were made.

Here is the King the Gentiles fear,
The Jews' most mighty King is here,
Promised to Abraham of yore,
And to his seed forevermore.

'Tis He the Prophets' words foretold,
And by their signs shown forth of old;
The Father's witness hath ordained
That we should hear with faith unfeigned.

Jesu, to Thee our praise we pay,
To little ones revealed today,
With Father and Blest Spirit One
Until the Ages' course is done.

Author: Prudentius (348-413). Translated by Allen McDougall.
Found in "Hymns of the Breviary and Missal," Britt, O.S.B.

Magnificat. In the Lydian mode 76
There are two Magnificats in each of the eight modes. This one has
been selected because it is one of the few examples of the use of the
pure Lydian mode. Notice the invariable final cadence on A. The composition is fugal throughout. The following Gregorian chant is intoned
at the beginning:

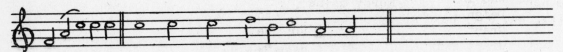

1.   Magnificat a - ni - ma   me-a Do- mi-num

The polyphonic treatment alternates with the chant according to the
numbers.

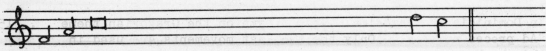

3. Qui-a respexit humilitatem ancillae   su-ae:
5. Et mi-sericor- dia ejus a progenie in   pro-geni-es
7. De- po-suit potentes de   se-de,
9. Sus-ce-pit Israel puerus   su-um,
11. Glo-ri-a Patri, et   Fili-o,

3. ecce enim ex hoc beatam me dicent omnes gene -ra -ti -o -nes.
5. ti - . - - - - - - - mentibus e-um.
7. et exal - - - - - - - ta -vit humiles.
9. recordatus miseri - - - - - cor-diae su-ae.
11. et Spi - - - - - - ri-tui sancte.

1. My soul doth magnify the Lord:
2. And my spirit hath rejoiced in God, my Saviour.
3. For He hath regarded the lowliness of His handmaid:
   for behold, from henceforth, all generations shall call me
   blessed.
4. For He that is mighty, hath done great things to me: and holy is
   His name.
5. And His mercy is from generation to generations: unto them that
   fear Him.
6. He hath shown might in his arm: He hath scattered the proud in the
   conceit of their hearts.
7. He hath put down the mighty from their seat: and exalted the humble.
8. He hath filled the hungry with good things: and the rich He hath
   sent empty away.
9. He hath helpen Israel His servant: being mindful of His mercy.
10. As He spoke to our fathers: to Abraham and to His seed for ever.
11. Glory be to the Father, to the Son, and to the Holy Ghost:
12. As it was in the beginning, is now, and ever shall be, world without
    end, Amen.

Lord have mercy on us
Christ hear us
Christ graciously hear us
God the Father of heaven, have mercy on us
Holy Trinity, one God, have mercy on us.

Holy Mary,   Pray for us
Holy Virgin of virgins
Mother of Christ
Mother most chaste   (Same response after each invoca-
Mother most amiable   tion down to the "Agnus Dei")
Mother most faithful
Virgin most merciful
Refuge of sinners
Comfortress of the afflicted

Queen of Angels
Queen of all Saints

Lamb of God, who takest away the sins of the world, have mercy on us.

Offertories:

Praise ye the Lord, for He is good: sing ye to His name, for He is sweet: whatsoever He pleased, He hath done in heaven and earth.

Exaltabo Te 177
        In the Ionian mode.
        I will exalt Thee, O Lord, for Thou hast upheld me, and hast not made mine enemies to rejoice over me: O Lord, I have cried to Thee, and Thou hast healed me.
                    (Translation from the St. Andrew missal)

Improperium 172
    In the Ionian mode.
        My heart hath expected reproach and misery; and I looked for one that could grieve together with Me, but there was none: I sought for one that would comfort Me, and I found none; and they gave me gall for my food, and in My thirst they gave Me vinegar to drink.

Marc Antonio Ingegneri. Born at Verona about the middle of the sixteenth century. In the complete edition of Palestrina's works, vol. 32, there is a set of twenty-seven Responses for Holy Week, labeled doubtful. They have until recently been attributed to Palestrina. However, in 1927 Ingegneri's own printed work dated 1588 was found at a sale, thus proving erroneous their ascription to Palestrina.

6 Responses.   (The numbers refer to vol. 32 of the complete edition)

16. Una hora non potuistis 214
        In the Mixolydian mode.
        Could ye not watch one hour with me, (Matt. ch. 26, v. 40) ye who exhorted one another to die for me? Or see ye not Judas, how he sleepeth not, but maketh haste to betray me to the Jews? V. Why sleep ye? Arise, and pray, (Luke, ch. 22, v. 46) lest ye enter into temptation. Repeat: Or see ye not Judas,....betray me to the Jews?

18. Omnes amici mei 216
        In the Dorian mode transposed.
        All my friends have forsaken me, and my enemies have prevailed against me: he whom I loved hath betrayed me. With terrifying eyes they beheld me, (Cf. Job ch. 16, v. 10) and they struck me with cruel blows, ("   " ch. " v. 15) and for my drink they gave me vinegar. (Cf. Psalm Ch. 68, v. 22) V. They have cast me off among the wicked, (Cf. Job ch. 16, v. 12) and my life they have not spared.   (Cf. Job ch. 16, v. 14) Repeat: With terrifying eyes....cruel blows.